D1301184

sid-manifesto
Silkscreen on wooden board, 75 × 55.5 cm
m.9 (1978)

mangelos rarely put a date on his works. He understood the course of his life as divided in 9 ½ periods, according to which we can date his work when a more precise information is missing; we will follow this method in the pages of this book, indicating to which period (m.3, m.4, m.5, etc.) the work belongs, and providing a date when possible. mangelos used this "bio-psychological" interpretation of the cycles of life as an alternative to the notion of evolution, and progress. He also ironically explained with this method the differences between the early and the late works of other thinkers and artists, and even predicted the date of his own death, in 1987.

```
sid-manifesto
───────────────────────────────────────────────
```

```
there are often mentioned "two" marxs
"three" van gogs"several" picassos ѐtc.
between-earl the differences are thus stressed
between early and late phases of authors.
the conclusive attitudes
are often different even oposite
as if they belonged to different unities.

the explantation is simple.
it is in the unlikeness of the subject.
the material presupposition
for the unlikeness of the subjects
is changing of the cells in the organism.

cells renew themselves every seven years.
assuming the physiological information
i was taught at school in sid is correct
i should be tke 9¹/₂ mangelos.

mangelos no.1 .... 1921 - 1928
mangelos no.2 .... 1928 - 1935
mangelos no.3 .... 1935 - 1942
mangelos no.4 .... 1942 - 1949
mangelos no.5 .... 1949 - 1956
mangelos no.6. ....1956 - 1963
mangelos no.7 .... 1963 - 1970
mangelos no.8 .... 1970 - 1977  /assuming an app-
mangelos no.9 .... 1977 - 1984   roximate correc-
mangelos no.9½ .. 1984 - 1987    tness calculat./

1933,sid - 1987,les champs du dernier goulag
```

One Person with Two Faces
Ješa Denegri

Art raises endless questions, and although it would be reasonable to assume that advances in scholarship would put these questions to rest, it seems that this field generates ever more mysteries that evade resolution. Artworks whose existence was previously unknown emerge every day, and even known artworks may be improperly read or understood. It follows that the system by which we value art is subject to the same errors: perhaps some of the greatest artistic treasures are already before us, but unappreciated. Several decades back, a forward-thinking art critic spoke of "boundaries" lying "beneath the grass." What, and where, are the true "boundaries" of the art of our time? It is evident that they are not where the superficial eye seeks them. Maybe they are in those objects not readily recognizable as artistic, those objects that seem not even to ask that they be considered artistic. Everything, really, depends upon our readiness to identify with different objects, to accept or reject them based upon our own completely subjective criteria.

There is a strange-sounding word – mangelos – that relates to objects whose appearance and meaning are strange, as well. For those distant from this phenomenon, a word of explanation: mangelos is the pseudonym, derived from the name of a place near his hometown of Šid, that Dimitrije Mića Bašičević took to hide himself, and to discover that side of his personality preoccupied with creating objects. (To be clear, though, mangelos himself made no claims that his works were those of an artist.) As he worked, mangelos made no secret of his identity or what he stood for. We might easily say that in this sense he left no secrets, but such a statement perhaps only enlarges the secrets that have supposedly ceased to exist.

To those intimately connected to the art scene, there was a very well-known, "public" side to Mića Bašičević's personality: he authored the first monograph on Sava Šumanović[1] (which was in fact his PhD thesis), was one of the leading art critics of the 1950's (with fantastic essays about Lubarda[2] and EXAT[3], among many others), served as a director of the Gallery of Primitive Art in Zagreb and was one of the first theoreticians of "naïve" art, was a member of the editorial staff of the magazines Bit International and Spot, and managed CEFFT (the Gallery of Contemporary Art's Center for Photography, Film, and Television). For many, these would have been achievements enough. But simultaneously with his public activities, Bašičević was also mangelos, possessed of his own discrete artistic universe rather than projecting himself into the artistic world of others. The world of mangelos materialized gradually, one might even say unintentionally, between the years of 1968 and 1972, through the exhibitions Biljana Tomić organized in Belgrade and Novi Sad. This world took on a more definite shape at the 1977 Gorgona retrospective in Zagreb, and at mangelos' own retrospectives at Zagreb's Prostor proširenih medija [Space for Expanded Media] and Belgrade's Gallery Sebastian, in 1981 and 1986, respectively.

What is the relation between Bašičević and mangelos, public and private facets of the same personality? We may be certain of one thing: those two sides are inseparable. A man is all he carries within himself – a unity, even if a unity of opposites. Even before he became an art historian and an art critic, Bašičević felt compelled to find himself in his artistic work; his instinct eventually led him to specific issues in the history and theory of art. His decision to thoroughly research Šumanović's œuvre was not made out of a sense of obligation to a fellow artist from Šid – or if it initially began as such, deeper insight transformed Bašičević's affinity for the great and ill-fated painter's work into something else. He drew closer to the issue of those schisms that inevitably exist in the artist's spirit, in his soul.

Much can be said of Šumanović, but one thing immediately springs to mind: he was an artist who, consciously or not, had set himself on a path toward the "obliteration" of his knowledge (knowledge gleaned from books, Parisian museums, and André Lhote's academy), so as he reached the end of his road he achieved the originality of a somewhat naïve artist ("naïve" in the positive sense of the word, of course). Could Bašičević's interests in Šumanović and in naïve art then be connected? Both his study of Šumanović and his development of a critical theory of naïve art led him to the following conclusion: when we speak of man's compulsion to create, we speak of something completely original, fundamental, preliminary. That "something," one keeps hidden within himself, and it must be drawn out into the light at any cost.

And literally out into the daylight – because he worked primarily at night – did Bašičević began bringing mangelos' ideas: first primarily in numerous personal notebooks he had never shown to anyone, and later, in objects that today seem unique phenomena of contemporary Yugoslavian art. Unique not only because of their content, which remains difficult to read and interpret, but also because of its evidence of one man's search for "something" all his own. Bašičević's night work, under mangelos' signature, is "private," although never confessional; philosophical rather than poetic; and on occasion, as much "wise" as it is elementary, like the writing of a person (whether old or very young) who has just learned his first letters. Those objects of mangelos seem to represent at once the obliteration and sublimation of Bašičević's knowledge: at first glance, these objects lack sophistication, but closer examination reveals them as the work of someone of great erudition.

It is not accidental that the emblems of mangelos' work are schoolroom objects such as notebooks, slates, and globes, and that on these schoolroom objects appear words in the unsteady and uncertain hand of someone who seems only recently to have begun using a pen or chalk. Bearing in mind Bašičević's attraction to naïve art, it is worth mentioning that he was the son of Ilija Bosilj, one of the most authentic self-taught artists. The relation between Bašičević's taste for the naïve and mangelos' so-called "tabulæ rasæ" seems a link whose causes and consequences are unknown. mangelos' artworks look like the exercises of an elementary school pupil only until one scratches more deeply into their content. And herein lies the real difficulty in interpretation, for mangelos' writings comprise very complex, ambiguous, partly ironic and partly serious sentences – sometimes encompassing whole stories about art and its history. It is obvious that these writings

pp. 54–57

were produced by someone with a tremendous facility for historical and philosophical consideration of art, but at the same time this individual seems to have suffered a gradual loss of confidence in the power and utility of such reflection. At the moment Bašičević concluded that almost nothing important can be said about art with a common and rational language, mangelos appeared to cobble together what few useful words remained into idiosyncratic statements about art. mangelos' messages are hermetic, cryptic, often written in several intertwined languages (French and German, Serbian and Croatian), and awkwardly spelled. Despite the obscurity of these messages, mangelos' intention is quite clear and he is unmistakably critical of the art of the past, and of such charismatic modern artistic personalities as Picasso and the like. mangelos' writings are an extended commentary on the meaning of art and its lack of meaning, and he did not restrict his attention to those works most easily and directly labeled as art. It is therefore unsurprising that Bašičević-mangelos carefully avoided publicly referring to himself as an artist: as Bašičević the art critic, he intentionally distanced himself from art through discourse, and as mangelos he wrote and spoke in a mute (zauman[4]) language that might, for its muteness and lack of need to label itself, be considered the language of art itself.

mangelos' work, on the border between the pictorial (visual) and the literary (textual), is not just for viewing: it demands to be read, like poetry or prose. For this reason it is not possible to evaluate these pieces only according to their shape, genre, technique; it is necessary to delve into their contents, meanings, and messages. Most often these works incorporate sentences or stories (or more accurately, "no-stories") in which the conventions that characterize the field of contemporary art are ridiculed, but other issues present themselves as well, ranging from everyday "truths" to morality and politics. These texts, however, written in a hand that mimics that of a first-grade student, are not so benign as they might seem at first sight: they are bitter, sometimes destructive in their undisguised cynicism. It seems the aphorisms of the artist mangelos were the art historian Bašičević's way of undermining at once the established hierarchies of the art world and society. The whole gamut of those less conspicuous, "minor" works is the underside of monumental and "great" art; according to mangelos, in primers and high-school notebooks there is more familiarity and warmth, more wisdom than in encyclopedias and academic treatises. Learning one's first letters (Azbuka[5] and Alphabet) and setting down elementary knowledge (such as the Pythagorean theorem) in writing are small undertakings applied to the symbolic tabula rasa – but mangelos does not specify whether these slates are blank before or after a lifetime's cognition.

Whether intentionally or not, mangelos' work to this day resists easy placement within the context of the art of its time. mangelos originated at the time of the war and worked in secret until the 1950s, at which point he began at least to find his artistic footing, if no peers, nor any artistic milieu to speak of. His artworks would further come into their own under Gorgona, a group in which mangelos participated for a time – if it is possible to speak here of a group, or of belonging, at all. Members of Gorgona[6] (Gorgonaši) revealed very little to one another, and mangelos was strictest in this sense: he associated with them, but he showed them so little that even they had no clue of his objectives until the Gorgona retrospective in 1977. But if there is anything remotely similar to mangelos, it could only be Gorgona, with which he was aligned spiritually, intellectually, and behaviorally.

In keeping with his simultaneous identification as a dual (Bašičević-mangelos) and discrete (Bašičević = mangelos) personality, mangelos was an extremely well-educated individual who, in order to shield himself from the world and preserve his inner tranquility, sometimes intentionally took on a childlike persona; this public figure turned inward, seeking refuge from public conflicts in a place where his intimate fictions ruled. mangelos' irony, skepticism, icy peace and passive resistance, made him a "Gorgona" spirit par excellence. In many particulars his behavior towards his Gorgona fellows typified that of the group, but this behavior seems to have been a mask. Only his works reveal his true soul: that of a poet, a wise man, a person whose sensitivities drove him to art as a vocation which would fulfill his need to achieve complete spiritual (and ideological) autonomy.

Very specific circumstances enabled mangelos' work to be discovered, recognized, and finally, interpreted. Not coincidentally, mangelos' moment arrived within the time and context of the new art in the late 1960s and early 1970s, when the Yugoslavian art scene shifted its focus from the outward appearance of an artistic object to its maker's conceptual objectives. Without any intention or expectation that it would come to pass, mangelos emerged as an early advocate of the artist's book, of the text as an artwork, of the artwork as an appropriated object and, more generally, of personal, individualized mythologies in Yugoslavian art. From the historical perspective of an alternative narrative in contemporary Yugoslavian art, those very tendencies from which mangelos was initially distant have come to cast him as a central figure: the history of art from which Bašičević tried to escape today includes mangelos, who most probably would never have relied on that history. The shifting between private and public spheres has concluded, with the following result: he who attempts to escape art will only find shelter in it again. As was noted, correctly, in the introductory text of the catalogue for mangelos' Belgrade retrospective in 1986, time has resolved two authors into a single person, and brought to light mangelos, whose long-lasting fight against art finally became art itself.

1   Sava Sumanović (1886–1942) was a Serbian painter born in Šid, the native town of Dimitrije Bašičević. He went to Paris in 1920 to attend the courses provided by the cubist painter André Lhote, and acquainted Modigliani, Max Jacob and Kiki de Montparnasse. He went back to Šid in 1930 where, in 1942, he was arrested by the fascist croatian militia and executed among 150 hostages.
2   Peter Lubarda (1907–1974) was a Serbian artist who notably painted the massacre of Kraguvejac, commited by the German army in Serbia in 1941.
3   EXAT 51, an abbreviation for "Experimental Studio" was a group of artists and architects active in Zagreb in the 1950's, who advocated abstraction and the synthesis of all artistic disciplines. It is known as the main avant-garde group in postwar Yugoslavia.
4   We might translate *zauman* as coming from behind the brain, and therefore not subject to reason.
5   Azbuka is another name for the Glagolitic alphabet, and the acronym of its two first letters (Az and Buk).
6   Gorgona was a group of artists, architects and art critics, such as Josip Vaništa, Julije Knifer or Ivan Kožarić. It have been active in Zagreb between the end of the 1950's and 1966, although it became acknowledged only in the 1970's.

"But even in a poem which simply describes a landscape something
can be achieved, if the things created by men are incorporated into the
landscape. Cunning is necessary to spread the truth."
Bertolt Brecht, *Writing the Truth Five Difficulties*

In 1941 Dimitrije Bašičević had just turned twenty. Serbia had been
under German military rule since the invasion in Spring after its cities
were bombed. The family farm in Šid was a few miles away from the
German – and Italian – occupied border with Croatia. Before his father
decided to send him and his brother to continue to study philosophy in
Austria so as to escape from danger[1], Dimitrije Bašičević reopened his
school exercise books from before the war, and drew black squares in
ink on the blank pages of his French and German courses, or in
between the lines of his exercises in mathematics and rhetoric. This
inaugural gesture of the artistic work of Dimitrije Bašičević, not yet
mangelos, was not an aesthetic operation, but an act of mourning.
As he explains in his "introduction to no-art,"[2] his impulse was one born
of instinct: "in confusion i began to record death between the lines.
deaths. whenever i heard the news about neighbours, friends, cousins,
acquaintances going away never to return, i would mark it in black ink,
a black ink stain between the lines, without thinking, without purpose,
without explanation."

p. 20

His black squares, at first holes, tombs, obliterations, rapidly
transformed into writing surfaces, became blackboards: "i never
dared ask whom the grave belonged to. i ran away from questions and
graves. and returned to them. once i found a marked grave. it was the
grave of a man whose death was recorded by a black ink stain in my
notebook. it said: paysage de la mort de mida. mida was the name
of a teacher. he was a good man. why was the writing in french – i don't
know. later i put the same inscription on all those anonymous graves.
paysage de la mort."[3]

The margins of his notebooks filled up with these landscapes,
often commenting on the notes and copies of the lessons: Monday's
landscape, landscape of friendship, landscape of testament, landscape
of grammar, of the pluperfect... In the universe of war, speech is no
longer trustworthy: "in the time of dying the books smelled of death
too, and reading smelled of dying." (*introduction to no-art – triumph of
instinct*) "Ideas were pressing against one another like rams. Hate had
a sanitary pace [...] The world was all flags," wrote Henri Michaux at
the time.[4] "Most of the following texts," he wrote in the preface of
Ordeals, Exorcisms, the collection of his poems written during the war
years, "are in a sense exorcisms through subterfuge. Their reason for
being: to ward off the surrounding powers of the hostile world."
The landscapes in Bašičević's notebooks stand also as a place of
exorcisms as much as that of a counter education. They stand in the
margins of the space of learning of the canonic knowledge of European

culture, and Bašičević adopted the handwriting of the applied student, drawing lines on these new blackboards (as he wrote in one of his notebooks in 1953: "tabula rasa is my blackboard"). He did this to record the instinctive programme, deliberately and falsely naïve, to which he would hold fast, with an unwavering loyalty, for the whole of his life. It meant questioning the legitimacy of this knowledge, with an indignation toward the barbary that knowledge could not prevent, but also in the face of which it revealed itself to be bankrupt, and for which it carried full responsibility. The feeling of being betrayed by culture, by language, complicit in the horror through its use in warmongering speeches, was similar to that diagnosed in *Lingua Tertii Imperii, The Language of the Third Reich,* the journal written by the Jewish philologist Victor Klemperer during the Nazi years in Germany, who wrote about an "infected language". It was also the one described before him by Karl Kraus at the beginning of the First World War. Kraus, the editor and the sole author of the review *Die Fackel* in Vienna, held the press as being largely responsible for the escalation of symbolic violence, which paved the way for war. In 1913 Kraus wrote: "In the realm of poverty of imagination where people die of spiritual famine without feeling spiritual hunger, where pens are dipped in blood and swords in ink, that which is not thought must be done, but that which is only thought is unutterable. Expect no words of my own from me. Nor would I be able to say anything new, for in the room in which one writes there is such noise, and at this time one should not determine whether it comes from animals, from children, or merely from mortars. He who encourages deeds with words desecrates words and deeds and is doubly despicable. This occupation is not extinct. Those who have nothing to say because actions are speaking continue to talk. Let him who has something to say come forward and be silent!"[5]

The experience of war, that of living through "the last days of mankind" (Kraus) and of surviving it, implies a paradoxical relationship with language: infected, it is no longer worthy of trust, and silence becomes an act of resistance, of necessary retreat, even though keeping one's silence is impossible. Kraus' solution to this aporia was to use quotes as weapons, to repeat the speeches of death until they become intolerable, fighting with the language against the language of others.

Thus the blackboard becomes the place of the dialectic of mangelos: from the mute landscape of mourning, square one of the form, it becomes the starting point of a life's endeavor, a vital one, under the sign of death. "from the emptiness of despair something like thoughts began to emerge. but if this situation may be described as renaissance, the question of its ambiguity arises. why two 'roads', double states. two modes." (*introduction to no-art – triumph of war*)

The loyalty of Bašičević to this questioning would take the form of night-work, literally and figuratively. First in a separation of signatures: Dimitrije Bašičević pursued a career as an art historian, theoretician and critic, that would notably lead him to become the director of

pp. 49–52

a number of art institutions, and mangelos would sign the "landscapes" and all of the work that would follow: an artist's name for someone who maintained that he had never considered himself an artist, designating his production as "no-art". Negation, driving all of mangelos' pp. 54–59 work (whether it was the series of "tabula rasa", the *négations de la peinture*, the *Abfälle* [waste], the *antiphons*, the *non stories*) pervaded an art bound to be produced at night, and kept in the private sphere, that of family and friends, without an explicit desire to make it known to a wider audience, and certainly with no intention to make career, commerce or gain any kind of social status from it. "perhaps it should be emphasized that no-art primarily contains a personal version and a private program, or an effort to conceive a program, not as an expression of creative potential, but as an expression of impotence." (*introduction to no-art*)

mangelos' night is to be taken as a continuity, and not as a rupture: at night at his desk, the art critic continued to question art and history, but in the aphoristic, fragmented form that his writing took on when he adopted the specific style of the perpetual student mangelos. It recorded doubt, pessimism, irony and encryption. This is the meaning of the ambiguity that he mentions, of these "two ways" that he called p. 61 elsewhere "dilemma." It was no longer a question of writing for others, for publication, defense or affirmation, but only a question of recording for oneself, of naming, of repeating, of chanting. Philosophy and poetry are based on the same secret language: a re-founding of language, of the letter before the word. mangelos never stopped inscribing and repeating alphabets on his boards and in his notebooks, in a kind of pp. 62–63 copyist ritual: Greek, Latin and Glagolitic alphabets, the language of the first Serbian bibles of the Middle Ages.

The continuity between the work of Bašičević and that of mangelos is Heraclitian in nature, in the sense that it maintains a unity between the two sides of the world, the day and the night. ("All things come out of the one, and the one out of all things," fragment B10 of Heraclitus). This nocturnal aspect is to be exposed to death, an awareness of the finite that he experienced and from which his work originated. It was in the discord, completely interior, between night and day, that the unity of the work of mangelos was set, *polemos*, again in a Heraclitian sense: "What opposes unites, and the finest attunement stems from things bearing in opposite directions, and all things come about by strife." (fragment B8) As mangelos affirms in the globe entitled *le manifeste sur la mort* (c.1977–78): "there is no death. it is simply another form of life."

The language forged by mangelos systematically manifests defiance and discord by situating itself between languages: first Serbian and Croatian, that he considered one single language, spelling numer-p. 51ous terms according to improper pronunciations (the "paysage de chide" that spells *à la française* his birthplace of Šid, in this way unrecogniz- able). French, German, English are used with a feigned clumsiness as languages of school, languages of culture that have revealed them- selves to be languages of betrayal, and thus languages to be betrayed, through multiple ways. First of all, an handwriting that excludes all capitals and punctuation, making all propositions ambiguous, perma- nently uncertain when it comes to translating them into the language of standard communication. This strategy can be found, for example, in certain theatre plays by his contemporary Peter Weiss, where the systematic absence of typographical signs prohibits distinguishing words cited from the direct style of thinking transmitted in an indirect style. mangelos also used abbreviations, or neologisms by associating truncated words (thus, "fumiš" is the abbreviation of "funkcionalno mišljenje", functional thought), and numerous terms belonging to private language, made up of nicknames and puns, which are also abundant in Bašičević's correspondence. His intention is clear: no one has access to meaning in a transparent manner, and language cannot be – must not be – a functional tool, but rather a means for expressing experiences, feelings, which remain individual and untranslatable. Language was for mangelos the tool of corrupted power, in the service of ideologies designed to divide men. His idea was to fool it, to hijack it, so as to build an impure, hybrid and individual "persolect," not in the sense of a withdrawal, but of a starting point, a new origin from which to express oneself.

All of mangelos' work developed a philosophical point of view founded on historical pessimism, on the sensation of an irreversible split between the time of History and the experience of time, close in this sense to Walter Benjamin's perception of the "lack of experience" known to the survivors of the First World War, as they were unable to link their experience to the narrative of History. mangelos thus de-scribed a radical dichotomy between what he calls "emotional thought" and, alternatively, "instrumental" or "functional" thought. In a brief manifesto, he wrote: "the term of sensory certainty and the like have no validity in the civilization of "extended" senses that is, through their instrumentalization. if emotional thinking is based on the sensory foundation their extensions form instrumental thinking."

So there are, according to mangelos, two civilizations, one that admits emotional thought, and one of "extended" senses that only tolerates an instrumental form of thought. These two civilizations do not coexist: one replaced the other in the human evolutionary process, and through it creates what we call History: "history is a special form of evolution modified à la humaine" (*manifesto on history no.1*). mangelos, considering History as an anthropomorphism of evolution, opposes these two civilizations, one that allows meaning, and is insep-arable from a sensitive perspective in and on the world, whereas the other only offers a process of rationalization with the goal of technical domination: "the functional way of thinking appoints function to the place held by meaning in the naïve way of thinking" (*manifesto on meaning and function*).

mangelos places this civilizational turn at the beginning of the 20th century ("functional thinking is a way of thinking the evolution of which is based on mechanical work and has started half a century ago," *manifesto on functional thinking no.1*). The notion of "naïve thought", which he claims is the condition for meaning, is similar to what numer-ous authors called for, after having faced a complete mobilization of their being in the service of war, leaving no place for meaning. This is expressed by the Dadaist writer Hugo Ball: "Zurich, November 25, 1915: [...] In an age like ours, when people are assaulted daily by the most monstrous things without being able to keep account of their impressions, aesthetic production becomes a prescribed course. But all living art will be irrational, primitive, and complex; it will speak a secret language and will leave behind documents not of edification but of paradox."[6]

p.70   The *homo naivus* of mangelos, very much like the primitive of Hugo Ball, are not to be considered as aesthetic genres, even if dada borrowed from African art and Bašičević was concerned with Naïve art in his role of director of the Zagreb Gallery of Primitive Art. This was also the influence of the work of his father, Ilija, an autodidact who began to produce naïve paintings at the end of the 1950's. For mangelos, *homo naivus* is "the type of man that in terms of evolution belongs to the civilization of manual work." His thinking, "ninety percent instinct (circa) and about ten percent rational thought," expresses itself in the related fields of "religion art philosophy" (*homo naivus manifesto*). The artist, like the philosopher, are *homo naivus* for mangelos, anachronistic in the technological civilization. Anachrony, also evident in the title of Hugo Ball's autobiography *Die Flucht aus der Zeit* [A Flight Out of Time], is the consequence of this feeling of rupture between the time that is experienced and the time of History that mangelos evokes, referring to the japanese legend of Urashima Tarō in the 1970 note-

pp. 104–105

book titled *model fm* [fm, another abbreviation of "functional thought"]. A simple fisherman, Urashima Tarō, is invited to the Water King underwater palace as a reward for saving his daughter. On his return he discovers that 300 years have passed unaware to him. Desperate at not recognizing anything of his life, he opens a box that the princess gave him along with a warning to always keep it closed. He instantly turns to dust, aging hundreds of years in the blink of an eye. In contrast to the necessary escape from historical time of Ball, mangelos experiences the anachronism of *homo naivus* as an inevitable, tragic fatality, but also as a form of resistance within functional civilization, which attributes nothing other to man than a role in society: "homo naivus has survived through evolution and history in a free-for-all ruthless battle. this way of existence has been verified in evolution as selection and in history as the chief instrument of achieving happiness, the common and generally accepted purpose of this existence." (*homo naivus manifesto*)

To better understand the ideas of "naïve thought" and "functional civilization" that he particularly developed in his work of the 1970s, which is more open to public expression (he notably published a number of pamphlets containing manifestos that he presented in the exhibition he organized of his own work in 1978 in Zagreb), it is necessary to see him as a contemporary of Hannah Arendt and Theodor Adorno, following on the philosophies of Martin Heidegger and, in particular, Edmund Husserl. It is above all, in parallel with the work of the Czechoslovakian philosopher Jan Patočka, also a contemporary, that light can be cast on a number of mangelos' ideas on History and the crisis of European civilization.

Patočka is known for being the author, together with Vaclav Havel and several other intellectuals, of the 77 Charter in Czechoslovakia, a petition that defined what implied the notion of dissidence. Despite the fact that Patočka and Havel made it clear that "modern civilization in its entirety", and not just totalitarian governments, was the subject of their criticism, the 77 Charter has been subject to misunderstanding and manipulation by western intellectuals, promoting liberal restoration under the cover of anti-totalitarianism. It was equally accused of being "anti-modern", in other words reactionary, a criticism that could be leveled at mangelos himself viewed from a certain angle. Patočka's criticism of modernity, shared by mangelos, is however located beyond the question of modernism: it is a criticism of the conception of history "centered around the autonomous subject that recognizes no higher authority, and its tendency to want to be both its own center and the pivot for the rest of being."[7]

Following Husserl, of whom he was a student, Patočka named *Lebenswelt* "the natural world" or "the life-world", which is the world where man realizes certain potentialities in his life. It is where his most authentic way of being is accomplished, that is to say his ability to relate to himself, to others, to the community, in a manner that is not simply utilitarian or functional, but rather in a way where questions of meaning, truth and responsibility become the horizon of these relationships. Patočka confronts the "life-world " to the sphere of everyday life, "the agenda" by which societies, whether they are democratic or totalitarian, exert power over individuals. According to Husserl, the European crisis comes from the forgetting of *Lebenswelt* through the technification of knowledge as a process that discredits all anchoring in the world of experience. For Patočka, access to the "life-world" is the condition for the problematic interrogation of the meaning of existence, the responsibility toward a community. It is through an action, a decision, that man, according to Patočka, refuses the shelter of daily life or of tradition, and exposes oneself to his finite nature, to death. This realization is the condition for being open to the problem of meaning, which Patočka identifies in Greek philosophy: "What made Greek philosophy the foundation of the whole of European life, is to have deduced from this situation a life project that transforms the curse [of finiteness] into greatness. On the condition, of course, that we make it the program of all human life."[8]

Openness to meaning comes from the conflict between the "life-world" and the "life for life's sake," i.e. the sphere of daily life, the regime of opinion, of obviousness. The "life-world" is for Patočka a preface, a background to all human destiny, and yet is not given to, or deductible from, its perceptions. It is thus in a series of "movements," of decisions, that Patočka sees this reunion of man with the "life-world." The first movement is that of *taking root* in the world: the creation of a home, belonging to a community. The second movement is "self-projection", reproduction, extension of oneself, which is at the heart of production, of work. It is in this movement that the functional dominates, where man falls into a role. "Things do not appear to him as themselves, but only as he is faced with them, where he forces himself to dominate them, so that they serve his project."[9]

The development of man's rational faculties is also a movement of giving up one's life, which fragments into a succession of moments occupied by providing for one's needs: it is "life for life's sake." The danger in thinking that this movement constitutes the finality of life, is what Patočka, like mangelos, perceives as a transformation of the world into a group of forces in the service of man, in a purely utilitarian manner, and ultimately demean man to the level of a cog in an uncontrollable machine of domination. The way that technified science intervenes in reality, "brings into play only one function of life, one that is distinctly impersonal, an objective function."[10]

So the possibility of ethics only appears for Patočka with the last of the three movements, one that he calls "breakthrough". Its decisive experience is about coming face to face with death. Being "startled by the finite" allows one to become aware of the first two movements as simple possibilities, and not as ends in themselves. "Only confront-ing the possibility of death, allows one to live, to rise above the vacuum of meaning that is dispersion in the alienating present. This discovery is not that of the nonsense, but on the contrary, is where freedom is rooted; this is where the world can appear problematic to us, and where the Other becomes the subject of our responsibility." This dis-covery is a struggle with oneself, against the tendency toward a life prepared to conceal any responsibility beyond that of our own survival; it is, according to Patočka, the fruit of an abandonment in regards to the vital movement that encloses and separates individuals, to establish a co-existence that he calls "the solidarity of the shaken."

The experience of war was the "breakthrough" moment for Patočka and mangelos, at the height of the civilization of domination of man over nature, and of man over man. "The movement through which man abandons himself to become lost in things, the 20th century has made this its constituting standard and its program: not only is our epoch characterized by the loss of the original ground where the movement of existence was accomplished, in its inherently human vocation, and not only will this loss not be seen, or felt as such, but will be implicitly held up as an ideal."[11] Just like mangelos, Patočka saw the 20th century as a rupture: "The 19th and 20th centuries form an era of industrial civilization that now seems to have definitively set aside other more ancient attempts by humanity to shape, even to make a life without the help of science or technology. [...] The result is an immense [...] rupture that allows certain people to consider the last three hundred years as barely the timid beginning of a true history of humanity, with the rest being relegated to prehistory."[12]

However this experience of the historical rupture of the "20th century as a war" that removes all anchoring, this awareness of non-sense is, paradoxically, opening up to the possibility of meaning: "What humanity, despite all of the difficult trials of history, does not want to understand, our late epoch, that has reached the height of destruction and ruin, will perhaps be the first to acknowledge: that life is to be understood, not on a day to day basis, with the sole idea of accepted life, of life for life's sake, but from the point of view of conflict, of the night, from the point of view of *polemos*.[13]

All of the spheres of "authentically human" activity such as art, thought, ethics and politics are established for Patočka through the struggle of everyone with oneself, which is the breakthrough to the world. In his dilemma between the instinct of *homo naivus* and the functional rationality of the "second civilization", mangelos, who had the original experience of being confronted with death and being exposed to the finite, never ceased the struggle with himself, the *polemos* of the diurnal and nocturnal aspects of life: in his dissatisfac-tion with the idea of performing roles, including the one of an artist, and the doubt he expressed through negation, he produced work as an "authentically human" activity, as a movement beyond that of survival, a movement toward a new beginning, the possibility of a different philosophy of history. His 'non-functional' thinking aimed at grasping what is the most real in the absurd. By understanding the tragic gap between ideas and emotions, he found ways for their possible reconciliation.

1   The three of them were actually sentenced to death by members of Ustaša, the Croatian Nazi organization which killed Serbs, Jews and Roms in the surrounding area of Šid that became part of Croatia.

2   "introduction to no-art" (1980), originally published in *Quorum*, issue 1, Zagreb, 1989, two years after the death of Dimitrije Bašičević.

3   The english translations of the manifestos by mangelos quoted in this text are taken from Branka Stipančić (ed.), *mangelos nos. 1 to 9 ½,* Fundação de Serralves, Porto, 2003. Translations from Croatian by Maja Šoljan.

4   Henri Michaux, "The March into the Tunnel" (1943) in *Selected Writings,* translated by Richard Ellman, New York, New Directions, 1968.

5   Karl Kraus, "In These Great Times", in Harry Zohn (ed.), *In These Great Times. A Karl Kraus Reader,* University Of Chicago Press, 1990.

6   John Elderfield (ed.), *A Flight Out of Time. A Dada Diary by Hugo Ball*, University of California Press, 1996.

7   Jan Patočka, "Comenius et l'âme ouverte", quoted in Alexandra Laignel-Lavastine, *Jan Patočka, l'esprit de la dissidence*, Paris, Michalon, 1998.

8   *Jan Patočka, Plato and Europe.* Translated by Petr Lom. Stanford University Press, 2002.

9   Alexandra Laignel-Lavastine, *Jan Patočka. L'Esprit de la dissidence.*

10   Jan Patočka, *Liberté et sacrifice. Ecrits politiques.* Edited and translated by Erika Abrams. Grenoble, Millon, 1990.

11   Alexandra Laignel-Lavastine, *Jan Patočka. L'Esprit de la dissidence.*

12   Jan Patočka, "Is technical civilization decadent, and why?", in James Dodd (ed.), *Heretical Essays in the Philosophy of History.* Translated by Erazim Kohák. Chicago, Open Court, 1996.

13   Jan Patočka, "The Beginning of History", in *Heretical Essays in the Philosophy of History.*

introduction to no-art
Dimitrije Bašičević mangelos
Extract from the text "introduction to no-art" written around 1980,
originally published in *Quorum no.1*, Zagreb, 1989.

triumph of instinct

there was a time when people were dying but there were no ideas. people died in masses, their lives violently ended. this was no fiction. it was completely different. completely different from all deaths in fiction. and in nature. different from all paintings, all songs, all news, and not like history. not at all. nor like life as we know it. it was the time of death.

in the time of dying the books smelled of death too, and reading smelled of dying. the books did not agree with what was left of breathing so you could hear the rustling of their paper lies in the silence of steps disappearing into death. i leafed through the notes i made in youth. what i heard was only the rustling of pages covered with empty words. in confusion i began to record death between the lines. deaths. whenever i heard the news about neighbours, friends, cousins, acquaintances going away never to return, i would mark it in black ink, a black ink stain between the lines, without thinking, without purpose, without explanation.

later, whenever i leafed through my notebooks it seemed to me i was in a graveyard. square black stains looked like graves. black, they stood out on white pages and the writing around them was like grass, grown and scorched. tall weed on a meaningless guard by anonymous graves. staring into nothing, i would often sit with my notebook in my lap. now and then i would turn a page, almost with fear. again a grave. again graves.

i never dared ask whom the grave belonged to. i ran away from questions and graves. and returned to them. once i found a marked grave. it was the grave of a man whose death was recorded by a black ink stain in my notebook. it said: paysage de la mort de mida. mida was the name of a teacher. he was a good man. why was the writing in french – i don't know. later i put the same inscription on all those anonymous graves. paysage de la mort.

20   *fragmenti ¾ 3*
Painted exercise book, tempera on paper sheets, 17.2 × 20.5 cm
m.3 (1935–42)

It is during the war time that Dimitrije Bašičević, who was 20 years old in 1941, reopened his exercise books from high school and started painting black squares on the blank pages. There, he painted his first "landscapes", most often commenting on the contents of his own assignments. It is remarkable that almost all of his later concerns already feature in these notebooks, and that he coined there the typical stylized and clumsy handwriting that he will keep in his later work.

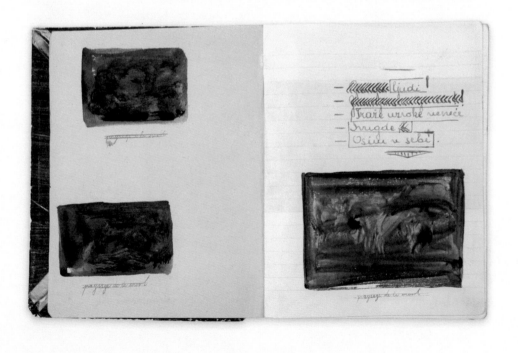

P R Í S A T E L J I

Sunce je blistalo u sjajnoj rasnosi
svoje svetlosti; opazivši ga tako sjajnog
i moćnog sunke izidoše iz mraka i pu-
žiše se pored njega ulazupiči se i namigu-
jući. Sunce se radosno nasmeši na njih
i oni sklopiše prijateljstvo.

Utom jedan cm oblak naleti na sunce i u jednom malu ga proguta, a prijatelji se razbegoše. Sunce se zakloua i polem-
se sure u obliku kišule maljica.

Jr. Nikorem
28. V. 39

(Ovo, ja nemam da li je
originalno. Možda je napisano u
inspiraciji. ~~~~~~~~~~~~~~~
~~~~~~~~~~~~~~~~~~~ Nepotreme

23

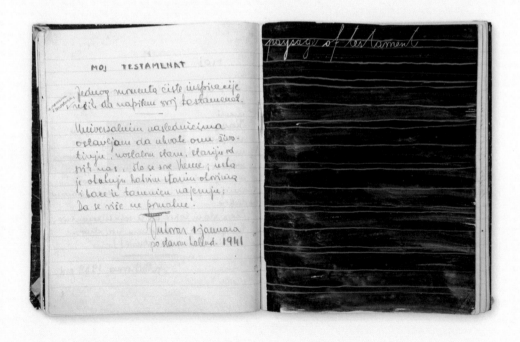

MOJ TESTAMENAT

Jednog momenta čiste inspiracije rešil da napišem moj testament.

Universalnim naslednicima ostavljam da uhvate onu životinje, moslalnu staru, stariju od svih nas, što se sve terne; neka je otaluju haljima starim olovnim i bace u tamnicu najemju; Da se više ne smalme.

Ulivar 1 januara
po starom koleud· 1941

poupaga of testament

FRAGMENT MOJE DUŠE

Ogromna je moja duša; i prazna je
moja duša. Zjape praznine bezobli-
čne i nepomate u beskrajnim uglovima
i struji hladnoća iz njih. A ona po
punjena mesta drhte usamljena
na hladnoći što se prostrá iz razja-
pljenih sredina; drhte i bojažljivo
se utiskavaju u sebe...
Tamo je onima koji imaju sićušne
male dušice ispunjene do vrha odre-
đenim tečnostima i poslaganim po
gomilice ... koji znaju danas šta
će biti sutra.

          Moja je duša večito lutorna
i nezadovoljna, večito gladna...

paysage de l'esperance

U OČEKIVANJU

Mi te čekamo. Priče
— (⊙. Papini.)

Misleći da si ti načinio njih i udahnuo
im dušu

Ali eto, to nije tako, nego oni su
načinili tebe, a sačuvali su ti uda-
hnuti dušu

Pa su te postavili na nekaki postament
i tamo te zazidali

Ti gledaš na njih svojim bezbrojnim
očima bespočno i tupo, ali ne možeš
da se kreneš

Nuja ti se očima u ruke i vija po svoj
volji, a ti gledaš, a ne možeš ništa
jer nemaš duše.

mi gledaju k tebi. Ali su daleko

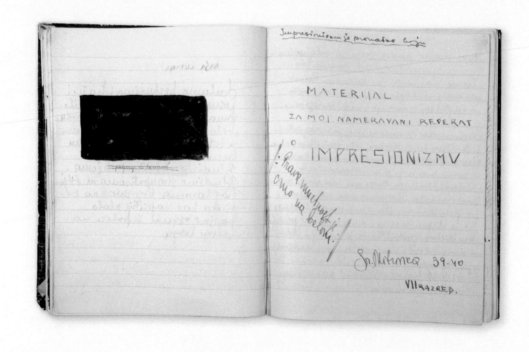

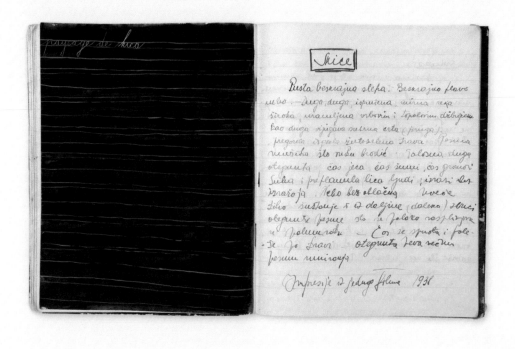

fragmenti 5. Kratak pregled sadržaja pročitanih knjiga
[Short review of the contents of the books I've read]
Painted exercise book, tempera on paper sheets, 17.2 × 20.5 cm
m.3 (1935–42)

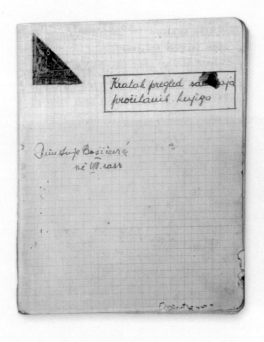

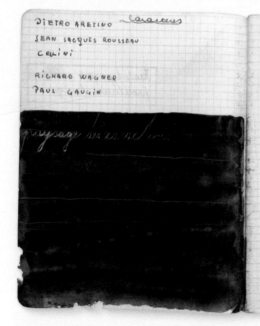

PIETRO ARETINO — *Caractères*
JEAN JACQUES ROUSSEAU
CELLINI

RICHARD WAGNER
PAUL GAUGIN

paysage

Eugen Kumičić   23.II.40
        Gospođa Sabina
glavna lica: Gđa Sabina, njezina kći koja
je pravi iskvarak svoje majke, njezine dvije
prijateljice Gđe Sabine Ivan Hribar i
Solarić koji zajedno sa glavnim licem
i jednim mladićem Nikolom Rišonović,
čine glavno obelježje romana ali bolje
rečeno čine kostur oko koja se obavija
život svega romana. Zatim nekoliko
mladića, jedna udovica i njezin nećak,
da bi bilo i pasivnih ličnosti i roman
potpuniji. ♦ (Ribčević, Vojnić, Senić, gđa Sabina Rišković)
Radnja se dešava u Zagrebu u vreme
vruće težnje za napuhanim svečano-
svim bankama i plemićkim titulama
Boja: naturalističko-realistična.
Sadržaj se vrti uglavnom oko gospođe
Sabine i njene kćeri torce koja je u
stvari nositelj radnje, dok ibol gđa

paysage

Antun Kovačić
Fiškal

27-12.40

D. ŠIMUNOVIĆ : TUĐINAC
P. ORSI : NOVA ITALIA
E. ZOLA : EXELENCIJA ROUGON
Б. ПОПОВИЋ : ОГЛЕДИ - II.
ANTOLOGIJA HRVATSKE NOVIJE LIRIKE
M. Crnjanski : LIUBAVU TOSKANI
VAN LOON : Povjest čovječanstva ma glasne
P. POPOVIĆ : JUGOSLOVENSKA KNJIŽEV.
ZLATKO MILKOVIĆ : B U DENJE (o Račiću D)
VINKO KRIŠKOVIĆ : ENGLESKI ESEJI
IVO HERGEŠIĆ : DOMAĆI I STRANI
S. Matavulj : Bilješke jednog pisca
H. IBZEN : SABLASTI
Moderna češka lirika
KRLEŽA : 3 kavalira gđe M. /Vrat
I. KOSOR RASAP
S. KRACEVIĆ : PESME

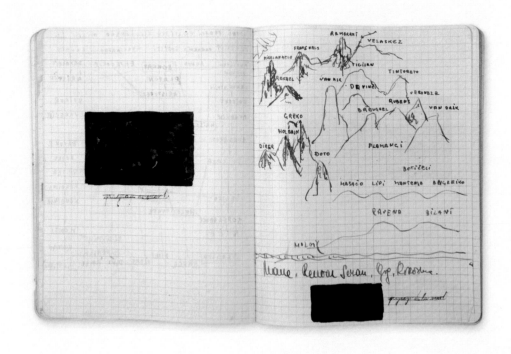

$$S_u = a_1 + a_2 + a_3 + a_4 + \ldots\ldots a_{n-2} + a_{n-1} + a_n$$
$$S_u = a_1 + (a_1+d) + (a_1+2d) + \ldots, (a_n-2d)+(a_n-d)+a_n$$
$$S_u = a_n+(a_n-d)+(a_n-2d)+\ldots a_1+2d+(a_1+d)+a_1$$

$$2\,S_u = (a_1+a_n)+(a_1+a_n)+(a_1+a_n)\ldots$$
$$2\,S_u = n(a_1+a_n)$$

$$S_u = \frac{n}{2}(a_1+a_n)$$

Interpolacija - Umetanje

$$a_{x+1} = a_x + d$$

$$\underbrace{a_{x+1}+\ldots+a_{x+1}}_{k+2}$$

$$a_{x+1} = a_x + (k+1)d_1$$
$$a_x + (k+1)d_1 = a_x + d$$
$$(k+1)d_1 = d$$
$$d_1 = \frac{d}{k+1}$$

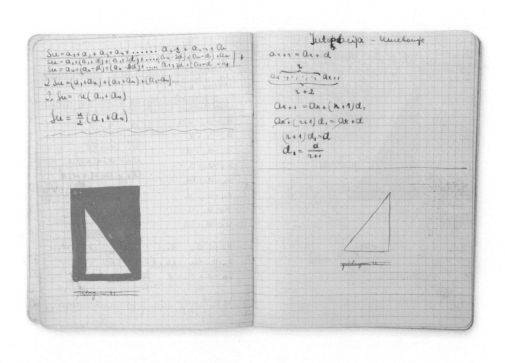

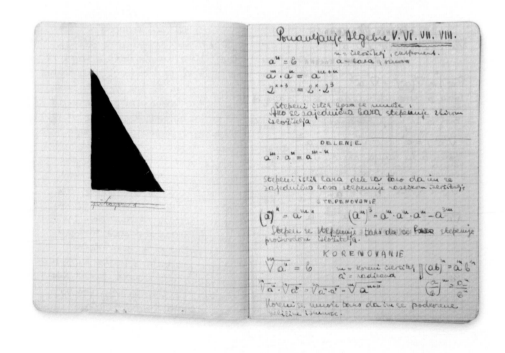

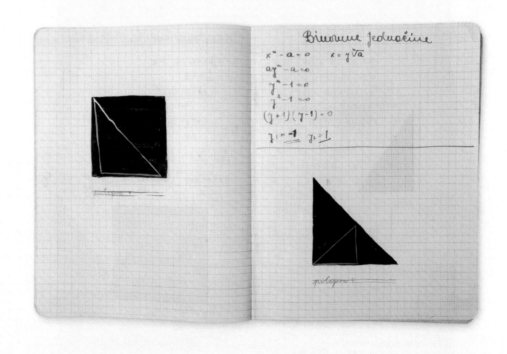

Binomne jednačine

$$x^n - a = 0 \qquad x = \sqrt[n]{a}$$
$$a y^n - a = 0$$
$$y^n - 1 = 0$$
$$y^2 - 1 = 0$$
$$(y + 1)(y - 1) = 0$$
$$y_1 = -1 \quad y_2 = 1$$

pitagora

manifest o društvu bez umjetnosti [manifesto on society devoid of art]
Silkscreen on wooden board, 62 × 45 cm
m.8 (1978)

manifest
o društvu bez umjetnosti
———

više od sto godina javno se raspravlja
o jazu izmedju umjetnosti i publike.
jaz se manifestira sve očitijim
slabljenjem interesa za umjetnost.
nadjeno je mnoštvo uzroka jazu
osim onog pravog.
uzrok je u civilizacijskoj razlici.
publika(društvo) mašinske civilizacije
prevazišla je tehnološka i ideoška
izražajna sredstva umjetnosti
koja su ostala na nivou prethodne civilizacije.

jaz izmedju društva i umjetnosti
nužna je evolucijska pojava
pa ima samo jednu tendenciju.
dalje produbljivanje.

manifesto on society devoid of art

there has been talk about the gap between art and the public
for over hundred years
the gap is visible in the increasingly obvious
lack of public interest in art.
this has been ascribed to many reasons
except the right one.
the cause lies in the civilizational difference.
in machine civilization the public has long surpassed
the technological and ideological means of expression
that remain at the level of the previous civilization.

the gap between society and art
is a necessary historical and evolutionary phenomenon
that has a single tendency.
to grow deeper and deeper

The Personal Mythology of mangelos
Ivana Bašičević Antić

A consideration of mangelos, his *no-art*, and his life, might begin with the "key" he embedded in a letter dated October 15, 1979. In that letter to my father (and the artist's brother), Vojin Bašičević, mangelos writes: "you can easily see that although the children[1] don't have munde[2] and they are not from džigura[3], they are intellectuals from the second civilization, in search of whose assumptions and dimensions their džigurian uncle is breaking his skull with, while alfa[4] snoozes under the table, on top of which the future dimensions of that civilization, which started a long time ago, should be outlined." Let me explain what the word "key" here means in this context. In his most elaborated essay, an analysis of his father's art, *my father ilija: a draft for an antimonography*[5], mangelos defines the term "key" in the following manner: "among the archetypes of his own art forms their author singled out one, nominating it as a key. In his opinion, all the other keys are contained within that one, i.e., all the other keys necessary for understanding his treatment of art." So the "key" is one of the archetypes present in his art, but is different from the others because it can be used to unlock the secrets of the whole of his œuvre. Further on, mangelos explains: "the key is the secret and the key to the secret at the same time."[6]

Džigura might prove the key to understand mangelos' art. Although my uncle predicted in another, earlier letter, sent to me just a few months after I was born, that the little I would learn of Džigura would come only from stories my father would tell me, as it happened, I spent a great deal of time in the house where mangelos was born – and so gained some firsthand knowledge of Džigura. It is the same house in which his father, Ilija (1895–1972), was born, lived, and died. Today, this house, in which he doodled in his first notebooks from high school, looks very much as it did when mangelos was a boy. But maybe it is better to start from the beginning...

In 1921 Dimitrije Bašičević was born to father Ilija and mother Mileva in the old family house in Šid, in the street the peasants used to call Džigura, and which was later officially renamed Vuka Karadžića Street. For Ilija and sons, Dimitrije and Vojin, Džigura forever remained the only name for their street. The ninth child in a large family, Ilija grew into the strong, determined, hardworking peasant mangelos characterized as a "despot patriarch":

"my image of our father from that period
is an image of a great powerful man
who struggled for his piece of earth and heaven
clever and self-confident
whose behavioral motives
seemed unfamiliar and strange
but whose orders were obeyed without question
this thought as an image refers to all the creatures
of that field including plants wheat corn and beet
granny ruža vojin seka neighbors relatives

in our household our father was a despot patriarch
for others only a patriarch"[7]

It should then come as no surprise that mangelos carried on a lifelong dialogue[8] with his father, from the time he first left the family home for the high school in Sremska Mitrovica, to his years at university following the war, and afterward when he had completed his studies and stayed on in Zagreb (where he would remain until his death in 1987).

The second "key" I would like to introduce here is the term *personal mythology* – not necessarily in the sense in which it is used in psychotherapy but perhaps I ought not to abandon that meaning altogether.[9] Attempting to describe the arcane, fictive worlds of artists, Harald Szeemann used the term "individual mythology", although maybe a distinction could be made between two categories embedded in this concept: those worlds that are invented and those that are appropriated and adapted. The first level of mangelos' personal mythology is the real-life world of his house in Džigura. The artist's life there was overwhelmingly defined by the despot patriarch Ilija, whose progressive vision extended well beyond what one might expect from a peasant. Whatever his undertaking, Ilija constantly strove for better and more advanced approaches: he employed the newest technologies in working his land, and he was among the first peasants in Šid to have a radio in his house. Most remarkably, and perhaps due to his own hunger for wisdom, Ilija did not expect his sons simply to stay home and work the family land; instead, he wished that they receive university educations. For Ilija, knowledge too was a form of progress. He read the books his boys brought home from school, and listened attentively to his sons' friends and later, their university colleagues. In an effort to make sense of life, human nature, the Bible and the church,[10] Ilija engaged such learned people as teachers, doctors, and priests in lengthy conversations.

The second level of mangelos' personal mythology consists of the names Ilija assigned to people, things, and animals based upon their surroundings:

"father inaugurated code language quite early
for home usage he first coded names
of all the acquaintances we frequently associated with
then many patterns of everyday life
question and answer patterns
i have forgotten most of them but i remember that when
a topic was to be evaded the answer was fossilized in
once upon a time there was an old hag or a frog saw horses being shod
so it held its foot out to the blacksmith irony was thus expressed
in most everyday conversation my father simply
transferred that irony to painting
so that almost every painting without a biblical or a rhyme book background meant
something special i.e. anything invisible which
could gain a visible trait entered his painting
in precisely that way
if the presumption is theoretically sustainable that painting is
the materialization of the invisible into the visible
a portrait of a painter's case would by all means be incomplete
without at least some pertinent details"[11]

mangelos here mentions coded language alongside of irony, that ever-present element of both his and Ilija's lives and communication. Irony served as an instrument of evasion of unwanted topics of conversation, but more interestingly, irony also became a critical element of both men's art. mangelos concluded that Ilija transferred irony to painting; at the same time, irony is maybe the only key to understanding mangelos' first globe, *paysage of al capone* (1952)[12] or the globe *krleža no.1* (1977–78).

p. 79

"Al Capone" was the unofficial nickname of academic artist Krsto Hegedušić, the influential figure on the Yugoslavian cultural scene who soon became one of Dimitrije Bašičević's first ideological enemies. At the time, Dimitrije was a young critic and art historian working as a curator in the Yugoslavian Academy of Arts and Sciences (JAZU), Hegedušić was a professor at JAZU, as well as a communist. Not long after he began working as a curator, Dimitrije realized the strength and airtightness of the circles of power within artistic institutions, and just how much sway those in power held. The artistic establishment decided what was art and what was not, allowing some artists to work, while making sure that the others remained invisible. In his search for artistic authenticity, Dimitrije seized upon the naïve art of Henri Rousseau and Ivan Generalić as "true" art, antithetical to its academic counterparts, which were devoid of both spontaneity and innovation. Dimitrije's promotion of this new and avant-garde art landed him trouble with the "boss,"[13] of course – and for the sake of his personal mythological order, mangelos created a new space, a globe, and called it *paysage of al capone*.[14] Of his use of globe as art object, he said: "... it was a thing that had a critical content, because at that moment i considered the earth to be a landscape of al capone, and we know who al capone was, so it has an allegorical meaning."[15]

Again using globes, mangelos satirized another important figure on the postwar Yugoslavian art scene: Miroslav Krleža, who is considered the most significant Croatian writer. For all Krleža's prominence as an author, it was his ideology that most influenced young intellectuals. His left-wing perspective cast him, in the eyes of the young generation, as a revolutionary, as a free, independent spirit. Krleža's novels were among mangelos' favorites when he was growing up – particularly *Povratak Filipa Latinovića* [The Return of Filip Latinović], which both he and Vojin enjoyed enormously as schoolboys. In the 1950's, Krleža was President of the Yugoslavian Academy of Arts and Sciences at the time that Dimitrije became Assistant Curator. His considerable sway in postwar Yugoslavia extended far beyond the boundaries of the cultural scene, and made a strong impression on the young man.

p. 4

"we speak of two marxes, three van goghs, and several picassos", writes mangelos in his *sid-manifesto* in 1978; the stylistic differences in these men's output from different phases of their careers are striking. In this manifesto, mangelos links creative development to the biological cycles whereby human cells are renewed every seven years. At its conclusion, he applies this concept to himself and separates his work into 9 ½ different periods – precisely predicting the year of his own death (1987). Two decades after his initial encounter with Krleža, mangelos subjected him to his artistic-philosophical theory of the divisibility of lives into phases, devoting a pair of globes – one of them blacked out, and the other white – to the writer. He inscribed the stand of his blackened Krleža globe with the title *krleža no.1* (referencing Krleža's first phase, which was his most significant), and on the globe itself he wrote: "der junge fritz (1893–1933)."[16]

Every bourgeois country in the Austro-Hungarian empire had its own "Krleža," mangelos had come to realize; Krleža's style was typically Austro-Hungarian, which therefore reduced the writer to "Fritz." Only the "young Fritz" produced anything of note, and young Fritz effectively "died" in 1933 – the year mangelos identified as the end of Fritz's first phase. It is worth noting several important events of 1933 that add multidimensionality to the irony in *krleža no.1*. In 1932 Krleža finished writing *Povratak Filipa Latinovića*, but according to mangelos the year's real milestone was the publication of Krleža's introduction to the book *Krsto Hegedušić, Podravski motivi – trideset i četiri crteža*.[17] This essay, which criticizes communist ideologues' need to dictate art and define aesthetics, ignited an ideological clash later known as "the conflict on the Left."

A globe describes a space without hard edges or endings; the color black is a negation. *krleža no.1* at once evokes Krleža's seemingly limitless influence and its limit. The endpoint mangelos assigns young Fritz's life does not signify an actual death, but rather, marks the death of mangelos' appreciation for Krleža's work. Furthermore, the subtitle "der junge fritz" is a nod to another writer in mangelos' library, James Joyce as his *Portrait of the Artist as a Young Man*.

The white globe *Kerleja I,II,II* (c.1979) presents three phases in Krleža's life: *Kerleja I*, *Kerleja II*, and *Kerleja III*. The object also evidences mangelos' penchant for playing with different languages. In this case, "Kerleja" is the French pronunciation of Krleža's name and this mispronunciation became an element of the artist's play – and of his irony.

Also instrumental to mangelos' development was Gorgona, of which the artist was a founding member. The group was named after mangelos' poem *gorgona*, itself named after the female creature from Greek mythology whose gaze turned to stone any man who looked on her. The mythological Gorgona is therefore interwoven with mangelos' personal mythology.

Today an internationally acclaimed artistic group, Gorgona, at the time of its inception in the early 1960's, was not specifically avant-gardist in focus. Rather, Gorgona was a small, informal collective of artists, art historians, and architects, and as in other areas of mangelos' life, in Gorgona, irony was central. Irony ran through the collective's art and their communications. Instead of issuing public manifestos, Gorgona's members exchanged humorous letters among themselves and with such like-minded figures as Piero Manzoni, Dieter Roth, and Victor Vasarely. Most of the major eastern European artistic movements of this period were connected with Gorgona. The terms neo-avant-garde, fluxus, neo-dada, conceptual art, void, artist's book, and mail art were all applied on Gorgona in retrospect by an art critic in 1977.[18]

By the 1960's, mangelos' attitudes toward art and society were steering him toward no-art and anti-painting; as an art critic, he gradually abandoned the conventional instruments of an art critic's work in search of new ones, better suited to new art, new civilizations, and new ways of thinking. On this new road, mangelos had no allies. At first he thought Gorgona would serve as a forum where his ideas would be understood and his work exhibited, but such was not exactly the case. mangelos was denied approval for his exhibition proposals "mutabor" and "fatamorgana," to be mounted at Studio G (a furniture shop in which Gorgona members organized exhibitions and discussed and criticized institutions). His proposal to put out a "non-issue" of the "anti-magazine" *Gorgona* (in its non-existence, the most Gorgona-like of any issue of the publication) was never realized. As a response to this slight, mangelos painted black the pages of a copy of the first issue (1961) of the magazine *Gorgona*, edited by the artist Josip Vaništa, and renamed it *Gorgona no.0.* Deeply dissatisfied, he at least realized that he had to go on alone. He was to find true understanding in Ilija and his art.

At nearly the same moment, in 1957, Ilija decided to take up painting, a pursuit he was to continue with a passion (if not an outright obsession) until his death. After a lifetime as a peasant and a farmer, Ilija lost his land and his vineyards to the communist government. mangelos described this loss as a turning point for Ilija, wherein he decided to divert his aggression: instead of the land, Ilija would cultivate the canvas – or paper, or wood, or any other material on which he might paint. Ironically, it appears that rather than unifying father and son, Ilija's art in fact caused the first major conflict between them. mangelos could not perceive his father's first artworks as art, and certainly not as fine art. Quite soon, however, mangelos would recognize Ilija's idiosyncratic paintings for what they were: windows into a truly unique artistic vision.

"here is one regrettable detail about the destruction of
the initial attempts of painting or drawing material
i know that it is unforgiveable to destroy such a collection
of the earliest i.e. first works and i destroyed them myself
convinced that father would not continue his work
this was definitely ilija's first phase started in 1957
it consisted of a few dozen drawings in pencil and pen
on our school notebook paper
the first drawing of st. cosmas and damian apart
the collection included drawings of horses and angels
winged figures in general
and the predominant subject was the nomadic life of gypsies
as far as the writer of these lines can tell
the drawings mainly resembled children's drawings
whatever information their analysis might have yielded
in relation to the opus it remains illusory all the drawings are destroyed
that was the first conflict between my father and me
in fact the first occasion that i committed something
that had never been on my mind
there is nothing further i would like to add about the conflict
except the incredible fact that it did not stop our father"[19]

That Ilija continued painting in the face of mangelos' resistance demonstrates his confidence and steadfast determination to become an artist. It seems he believed in art with a near-religious fervor. Did he perceive some form of magic in art? I think that he did – but ironically, I feel the same of mangelos and his art. Ilija filled his paintings with strange, two-faced or two-headed creatures floating or flying through spaces absent of perspective or gravity, that in no way resembled anything he saw in real life; mangelos employed archaic alphabets or incomprehensible words and letters as instruments in some sort of magic ritual, and never as a means of communication.[20]

In his writings about his father's work, mangelos uses an interesting expression for the otherworldly quality of Ilija's iconography – "enchantment." For mangelos, this was what Picasso, Mondrian, and Ilija were doing through painting: they were enchanting. Sometimes mangelos' paintings, on which we see the words *mutabor, fatamorgana, hlieb, otodra*[21], leave the impression that he too was enchanting.

A notable example of this magical procedure at work in mangelos' œuvre

p. 72

is *mon père ilija* [my father ilija] (1971–77). In the upper left corner of a wooden board painted black, mangelos has laid down a small square of gold leaf. Gold is one of the defining colors of Ilija's art, and more generally, gold connotes sacredness and value. Art historians assert that Ilija would have been familiar with the Byzantine convention of embellishing icons with gold; in keeping with this visual tradition, mangelos' golden square is an icon of his father, Ilija.

Going back to the term *personal mythology*, and to the series of mangelos' works incorporating words from Džigura, such as

pp. 74–75

la jighoura, el šegic, il monterosa, el cid: without help, the viewer of these artworks cannot decode the words written on them. These words are written in the Latin alphabet, whose letters are internationally recognizable. It would seem that mangelos wanted these words to be understood, but without a key, they have no meaning. Perhaps they are ciphers. Perhaps they are the puzzles of the world into which mangelos was born, and to which he belonged, spiritually, until the end. Monterosa was the horse his father nurtured and cared for until it died of old age. Šegić was the name of the dog – Ilija always kept one in the family house in Šid, but these dogs were each given one of only a few names, of which Šegić was most common. As a grown man, mangelos had a dog in his apartment in Zagreb. Ironically, he called it Alfa, the first letter of the Greek alphabet.

Alpha is a beginning. In order to escape the chaos and negativity that have pervaded our civilization since the outbreak of World War II (which took the lives of numerous relatives and friends), mangelos decided to start again from the beginning and thought everything had to start again from the beginning. This was the purpose of his *tabulæ rasæ*. There was no possible progress in a civilization capable of killing millions of innocent people.

In the autumn of 1942, the Croatian Nazi regime sentenced Ilija, Dimitrije, and Vojin to death. In order to escape their certain death they fled Šid, by train, to Vienna. This brush with death forever marked mangelos. It is often said of his art that it is pervaded by pessimism, and by an obsession with finiteness. It is for this reason that I would conclude this essay with an excerpt from mangelos' essay, *my father ilija*, in which he describes Ilija's death. Confronted with his father's death, mangelos was overcome by emotions he sought to suppress, but they are nevertheless present in his words. He considered emotion one of the fundamental aspects of Ilija's art, but in the creation of his own art, mangelos sought to work from intellect rather than emotion. He felt that there should be no aesthetic elements that might stir emotions, and yet, potential emotion hangs over all of his art – and still, he found himself, in the end, creating beautiful, handmade illuminations.

"while i was walking through the twilight of the dawn
to order a coffin from master hena's successor
for our father's funeral
still perplexed by recent moments
and by conflict of my own bewildered thought
with the feeling's persistence in the depth of my instincts
it is natural that i had to think about death
and about father

...

when i found myself among the coffins
i was relieved
for father for the deceased and all the dead of this world
there is no death
the living live for the living death does not exist
death exists neither for itself nor for the dead
for it is merely a pattern and nothing more
among its many models
life also made the model of death
as a pattern of one life form
if the thinking of the living is life
then in one moment
it calls itself death
one of its impulses one mechanism
for one of its metamorphoses of forms
my father's life was a metamorphosis
and his death another metamorphosis of those forms
death is the proof of life
and not the proof of its absurdity"[22]

1   mangelos here refers to a photograph of my brother and me.
2   A type of peasant sweater.
3   mangelos' childhood home was in the street colloquially called Džigura, in Šid, a small Serbian town near the border of Croatia.
4   The artist's dog.
5   Dimitrije Bašičević mangelos, *my father ilija: a draft for an antimonography*, Vojin Bašičević ed., Novi Sad, 1996, p.22. This essay was written in 1976–77.
6   Ibid., p.97.
7   Ibid, p.44. In this essay, as in many such essays mangelos penned after abandoning his position (and persona) as an art critic, there is neither capitalization nor punctuation, and very often single ideas flow from one line into the next.
8   Dimitrije and his brother Vojin exchanged numerous letters with their father Ilija. A portion of the three men's correspondence is reproduced in the Serbian edition of the above-mentioned book, *moj otac ilija – nacrt za antimonografiju*, Novi Sad, 1995.
9   In psychotherapeutic terms, personal mythology provides an individual means of escape from the chaos of one's life through the structure of an invented, mythological world.
10   Although Ilija rarely attended church, he did possess there his own table (in an Orthodox church, a personal space for prayer).
11   Ibid, p.48.
12   Now in the Städtisches Museum Abteiberg, Mönchengladbach.
13   It was at the very moment of this conflict between mangelos and Krsto Hegedušić that Ilija started to paint. So that Ilija might not be met with the same disfavor as he, mangelos advised his father to work and exhibit under the pseudonym Ilija Bosilj, and never to mention his last name. This ploy unfortunately backfired, touching off the so-called "Bosilj Affair," which culminated in 1965 when Ilija was forced to paint before of a panel of experts in order to prove that he was indeed the author of his paintings.
14   It was not mangelos who assigned the nickname Al Capone to Krsto Hegedušić; the name was already in informal use when mangelos created his globe
15   *Mladen Stilinović: Interview with Dimitrije Bašičević mangelos*, in: *mangelos nos. 1 – 9 ½*, Branka Stipančić ed., Fundação de Serralves, Porto, 2003, p.187
16   mangelos titled one of his no-stories "der alte fritz." [The Old Fritz]

17   This volume was a catalogue consisting of thirty-four drawings of Krsto Hegedušić and edited by Minerva nakladna knjižara, Zagreb, 1933.

18   The first Gorgona retrospective was curated by Nena Dimitrijević in 1977.

19   *my father ilija*, 49.

20   A similar impulse to demonstrate language's inherent failings, as well as ideological and other misuses of language by society, may be observed in the work of Marcel Broodthaers, who explored language's non-communicativity and non-transparency. In my doctoral dissertation, "Theory of Textual Practices in Visual Arts: Functions of Words and Images", I develop a comparison between Dimitrije Bašičević mangelos and Marcel Broodthaers on a postmodern theoretical platform.

21   *mutabor* means "I will be changed" in Latin: it is a magical word used in children's stories. *fatamorgana* comes from the italian sentence Fata Morgana and is a type of mirage; *hlieb* is the Old Slavic for bread, and *otodra* an Old Slavic word used in religious prayers.

22   *my father ilija*, p.58

49   *paysage de la mort* [landscape of death]
      Tempera on paper, 20 × 27 cm
      m.4 (1942–49)

50   *paysage de la deuxième guerre mondiale* [landscape of the second world war]
      Tempera on printed paper (geographical map), 65 × 45 cm
      m.4 (1942–49)

51 *paysage de chide* [landscape of chide]
Tempera on paper, 20 × 14.3 cm
m.5 (1949–56)

Chide is a deliberate misspelling of Šid, Dimitrije Bašičević's hometown in Serbia, as if that city was not Serbian but French. Typical of mangelos, this type of pun between languages aims at confusing and obscuring meanings, and at deconstructing the feeling of belonging.

52   *paysage* [landscape]
      Tempera on printed paper, 23.1 × 30.7 cm
      m.5 (1949–56)

54 *tabula rasa (2 – serie α)*
Tempera on cardboard, 27.8 × 21.5 cm
m.5 (1949–56)

The blackened surfaces of mangelos' tabulæ rasæ could be confused with monochrome paintings, in the modernist sense of an achievement of abstraction. mangelos obviously refers to Malevich's suprematist black squares, and especially to his attempt to escape from historical time. His intention is for the most part to provide for himself the conditions for a new start, an empty blackboard on which a new text can be written again.

55　*tabula rasa (4 – serie α)*
Tempera on cardboard, 27.8 × 21.5 cm
m.5 (1949–56)

56   *tabula rasa*
Acrylic on hardboard, 110 × 75 cm
m.5 (1949–56)

57 *tabula rasa*
Acrylic and tempera on cardboard, 21.5 × 28 cm
m.5 (1949–56)

58 *négation de la peinture* [negation of painting]
Tempera on printed paper, 23.7 × 16.7 cm each
m.5 (1949–56)

mangelos used to paint on whatever material he could find in his office
when he was working at night on his artistic work. The blackening of the
pages here reveals fragments of photographs reproduced in an art-
book from which he tore out some pages. mangelos consistently developed these "negations of painting" in the 1950's, although crossed-out
drawings and sketches already appear in his exercise books.

61   *dilema* [dilemma]
Tempera on paper, 24.4 × 18 cm
m.8 (1970–77)

g-alphabet
Tempera on canvas book covers, 27.3 × 18.5 cm each
m.5 (1949–56)
Private collection, USA

Prior to the creation of the Cyrillic alphabet, the Glagolitic alphabet was used from the IXth century in the Balkans and Central Europe for the copy of religious books and liturgies. It derived for the most part from the Greek letters, with ornamentalized designs. Each of the Glagolitic letters has its own symbolic meaning, its alphabet therefore being an encrypted sacred message.

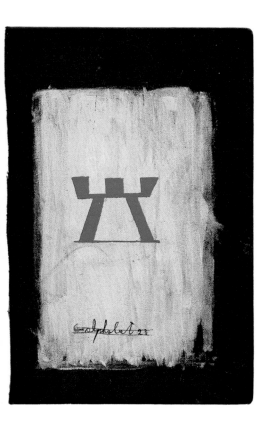

64 *paysage* [landscape]
Tempera and ink on printed paper, 19×27 cm
m.5 (1949–56)

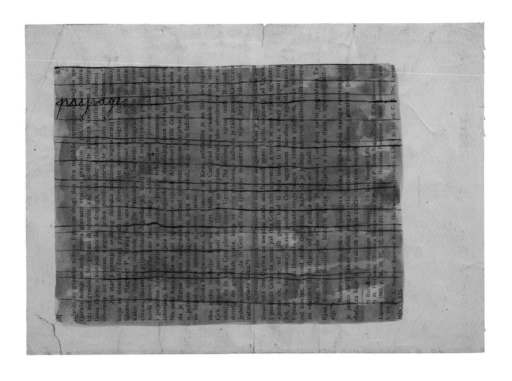

65   *paysage* [landscape]
Tempera and ink on printed paper (art auction catalogue) 16 × 23.2 cm
m.5 (1949–56)

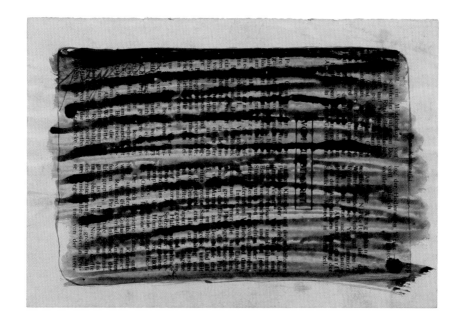

66   *Američka pesnikinja Gertrude Stein često je podsećala Picassa...*
[American poet Gertrude Stein often explained to Picasso...]
Tempera and collage on cardboard, wooden frame, 30.5 × 45 cm
m.7 (c.1967–72)

Gertrude Stein, the American poet, often explained to Picasso the meaning of things. She taught him how to observe the world with simplicity and open-mindedness. The portrait of Gertrude Stein shows her as someone simple, tall and strong. Her person physically fulfills the painting as much as she fulfills it with meaning.

a.schug

r.garaudy

Picasso operates a major turn between 1906 and 1907. We could say the beginning of this era was marked by the portrait of Gertrude Stein. It is significant that Gertrude Stein and her brother claimed satisfaction after she posed for the first time. Nevertheless, Picasso required ninety more posing sessions, and then erased everything he had done and left for several months to the countryside. Upon his return and in the absence of his model, he painted her portrait; when Gertrude Stein in a state of shock asked him if the painting resembled her, Picasso quietly answered: "you will one day". It is more than an anecdote: it is his conception of painting and his relationship to reality.

information
upon which theories and stories are based
are not reliable
by way of consequence theories and history
lose their utilitarian value
with the kind of information
which produces legends
instead of history
a mythology is born
and instead of a ~~reliable~~ critical analysis of
the activity of a man about whom we don't know if he went
to jail in the old days for his resistance or for his ideas
but about whom we know that he never stopped playing since his childhood
even the marxist critics create the myth of the rebellious hero
the hero of ideas
the genius

68   *picassov način mišljenja i heidegerov*
      [the way of thinking of picasso and heidegger]
      Oil on cardboard book cover, 14 × 22 cm
      m.7 (c.1967–72)
"the way of thinking of picasso and heidegger
is artistic or impulsive
this way of thinking always shapes the individual system
and closes itself in this system
whose codification is hidden through numbers
ungraspable to the logic of the author"

69   *picasso joyce eliot heidegger*
        Oil on cardboard book cover, 14.5 × 20 cm
        m.7 (c.1967)
"picasso, joyce, eliot, heidegger
do not produce thoughts
but commodities
exclusively of market value
deprived of the ability to communicate with the regenerative part of the world"

70   *homo naivus*
     Tempera on paper, 18 × 14.7 cm
     m.8 (1970–77)
     "the role of olfaction
     in the (for) naïve thinking
     what to do with a double morals"

homo naivus manifesto

homo naivus
is the type of man that in terms of evolution
belongs in the civilization of manual work.
the existence of homo naivus is characterized by
manual production
and naïve thinking.
the naïve way of thinking is constructed
of ninety percent instinct (circa)
and about ten percent rational thought.
characteristic of naïve thinking
are religion art and philosophy.

homo naivus has survived
through evolution and history
in a free-for-all ruthless battle.
this way of existence
has been verified in evolution as selection
and in history
as the chief instrument
of achieving happiness
the common and generally accepted purpose
of this existence

72　　*mon père ilija (1895–1972)* [my father ilija (1895–1972)]
　　　　Tempera and gold leaf on wood, 29 × 24.4 cm
　　　　m.8 (1970–77)
"my father ilija (1895–1972)
first sketch for the portrait – m.8"

　　　　　　　　The portrait evoked here by mangelos is the essay *my father ilija – draft*
　　　　　　　　for an anti-monography (1976–77) that he dedicated to his father, a
　　　　　　　　prolific painter in the last years of his life until his death in 1972. Partly
　　　　　　　　a poem and a philosophical essay, his draft is as much a testimony
　　　　　　　　of a son on his father, as an essay of the art historian who was already
　　　　　　　　a specialist of naïve art. But it is also a dialogue between two self-
　　　　　　　　taught artists, where it is unclear if its author is the art critic Dimitrije
　　　　　　　　Bašičević or the artist mangelos.

73   *paysage ugovora* [landscape of the contract]
Tempera on printed paper (Ilija Bašičević's agricultural contract), 31.2 × 23.7 cm
m.4 (c.1947)

74 *la jighoura (nomina 1)*
Tempera on printed paper, 27.3 × 35.5 cm
m.6 (1956–63)

In the *nomina* series, several names are invoked with capital letters
stenciled on a red background. Here mangelos is amused by their
resemblance with other languages and their estrangement when associated to a foreign article, borrowed from Spanish or Italian. In this
disguise, he can publicize words that come from his private sphere, like
"monterosa", the name of his father's mare in the family farm in the
city of Šid, on Džigura Street, here altered in "la jighoura" (as if spelled
in French). These puns were most probably part of the family folklore.
They are common in the work and correspondence of mangelos,
who liked to play with words and expressions whose meaning he would
keep private and out of reach.

il monterosa (nomina 5)
Tempera on printed paper, 27.3 × 35.5 cm
m.6 (1956–63)

77   *kad mlidijah umreti* [when i thought i would die]
Tempera on hardboard, 65.5 × 79 cm
m.6 (1956–63)

négation de la peinture [negation of painting]
Tempera on paper, 35.4 × 27.4 cm
m.5 (1949–56)

79   *krleža no. 1*
        Acrylic and tempera on globe made of wood, metal and paper, 22 (d) × 29 (h) cm
        m.8 (c.1977–78)
"the young fritz"

die energie [the energy]
Acrylic on wood, 40 × 40 cm
m.8 (1977)

81   *le manifeste sur la machine* [manifesto on the machine]
      Acrylic and Letraset letters on globe made of wood, metal and paper,
      36 (d) × 46 (h) cm
      m.8 (c.1977–78)
"the machine is the first model of functional thinking"

82   *theory of memory*
      Acrylic paint on laminated board, 39 × 29 cm
      m.8 (1970–77)
"theory of memory
resolves the problem of the spirit
and the body and soul dichotomy"

84   *termin čulne izvesnosti i slični...* [the term of sensory certainty...]
Tempera on paper, 20.9 × 19.9 cm
m.8 (1970–77)

"the term of sensory certainty and the like
has no validity in the civilization
of "extended" senses
that is, through their instrumentalization
if emotional thinking is based on the sensory foundation
their extensions form instrumental thinking"

85   *komentar razvijanju ideje* [a comment on the development of ideas]
         Tempera on paper, 21 × 20 cm
         m.8 (1970–77)
"a comment on the development of ideas
ideas are simple as are phenomena
they are expressed in short sentences
the so-called development of thought
is in fact fuzzy thinking"

86   *pithagora* [pythagoras]
Tempera and oil on canvas book cover, 31 × 22 cm
m.5 (1949–56)

Since his first drawings in his exercice books, mangelos referred
to geometry and more precisely to the scientist Pythagoras, who was
allegedly the first in Ancient Greece to claim that he was a philosopher.
mangelos probably liked that Pythagoras hasn't left a single line
of writing. The philosopher is for him the symbol of a rational thought
allied with a moral wisdom, long before the civilizational turn which
converted the reason into an instrumental and domination process of
man over nature.

87   *pithagora* [pythagoras]
Pastel and ink on cardboard, 30 × 23.8 cm
m.5 (1949–56)

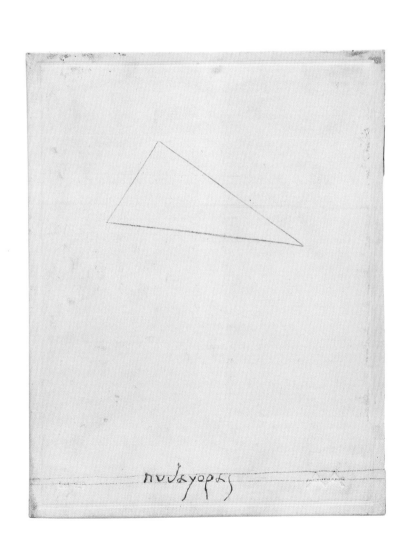

graficon
Tempera on printed paper, 23.7 × 16.7 cm each
m.5 (1949–56)

89 *grafikon*
Tempera on printed paper, 19.2 × 28 cm
m.5 (1949–56)

90   *grafikon*
Tempera on printed paper, 23.7 × 16.7 cm
m.5 (1949–56)

91 *noart 12. juna 1964*
Tempera and ballpen on paper, 12 × 10.5 cm
m.7 (1964)

"the most philosophical and most theoretical explanation of no-art is no-art", mangelos used to write. After he had broken the privacy of his practice with the first actual exhibition he organized of his work in 1971 in Novi Sad, he assumed that "a century and a half after hegel there is no need to act like a prophet, or a herald of no-art, but an attempt, albeit clumsy, to think in a new mode might not be a crime. perhaps it should be emphasized that no-art primarily contains [...] an effort to conceive a program, not as an expression of creative potential, but as an expression of impotence." (in *introduction to no-art*, 1980)

92 *paysage de mangelos* [landscape of mangelos]
Oil on wood, 20 × 25 cm
m.6 (1956–63)
"landscape of mangelos
you who pushed the mammoth mamat
to start singing
like the nightingale of the chinese emperor"

Here, the nickname mamat refers to the writer and art critic Marijan Matković, who criticized in the press the book that Dimitrije Bašičević wrote on the naïve painter Ivan Generalić.

93   *mane tekel fares*
Acrylic and tempera on globe, 35 (d) × 58 (h) cm
m.9 (1987)

mangelos' last work was dedicated to the fall of Babylon. "Mane, Tekel, Fares", are the words that an invisible hand writes on the wall of the king's palace, as it is recalled in the Book of Daniel in the Bible.
They mean "counted, weighted, divided" and announced the fate of the people of Babylon, and the doom of their kingdom. The expression generally implies that the future is predetermined.

manifest manifestah [manifesto of manifesto]
silkscreen on wooden board, 62 × 45 cm
m.8 (c.1977–78)

manifest manifestah

───────────────────────────────

dragi prijatelji
dragi neprijatelji

ovdje se ne manifestira iskaz
da je dugogodišnje eksperimentiranje uspjelo
jer nije
 već da je uočen drugi pravac kretanja.
umjesto po liniji smisla
proces mišljenja se kreće
po liniji funkcioniranja
adekvatno ostalim organskim procesima.
u tom okviru se kreće i materija manifestof.

svijet ne samo što se mijenja već se izmijenio.
nalazimo se u drugom stoljeću
druge po redu civilizacije. strojne.
društvenom upotrebom stroja
završena je civilizacija ručnog rada
a s njom i svi društveni fenomeni
čija je pretpostavka bio ručni rad.

izmijenivši karakter rada
svijet mijenja način mišljenja.
revolucija mišljenja ima karakter
dugogodišnje evolucije.
u toku tog procesa dojakošnje naivno mišljenje
ušlo je u proces zamjene s drugim mišljenjem
koje se osniva na principima mehaniziranog rada.

praktično se druga civilizacija profilira
kao kulturna organizacija medjuplanetarnog tipa
s jednoobraznom mašinskom proizvodnjom
i superstrukturama na kxxi principima
društvene funkcionalnosti.
umjesto emotivno strukturirane jedinke
formira se tip društvene jedinke
strukturirane funkcionalno.

manifesto of manifesto

dear friends
dear fiends

this is not a manifest claim that the experiments
carried out over the years were entirely successful
because they were not
but that another route has been discovered
instead of following the line of meaning
the thinking process proceeds
along the line of function
corresponding to other processes of life.
this is the framework for my manifestos.

the world is not only changing it has changed.
we are in the second century
of the second civilization. the machine one.
the social use of the machine
has put an end to the civilization of manual work
and to all the social phenomena
rooted in manual work.

by changing the character of work
the world changes its way of thinking.
the revolution of thinking has the character
of a long-term evolution.
in the course of this process the previous artistic or naïve thought
has integrated itself in the process of application with another one
based on the principles of mechanical work.

civilization is practically evolving
into a cultural organization of the interplanetary kind
with uniform mechanical production.
and consequently with uniform types of social superstructure
based on the principle of social functionality.
instead of emotionally structured units
a type of social unit is formed
which thinks functionally.

97   *mon père ilija* [my father ilija]
         Painted notebook, 16.5 × 11.5 cm
         m.8 (1972)

98   *comentari* [commentary]
Painted notebook, 16 × 11 cm
m.7 (1966)

"1. the main impediment to the elaboration
of the functional way of thinking
is the old way of thinking, which is unavoidable (a)
with its elements it will overload
the new one (b)
2. the next nuisance will come from
the confused limits between
the functional thinking
and the language
3. looking for physics beyond the psychobiological laws should..."

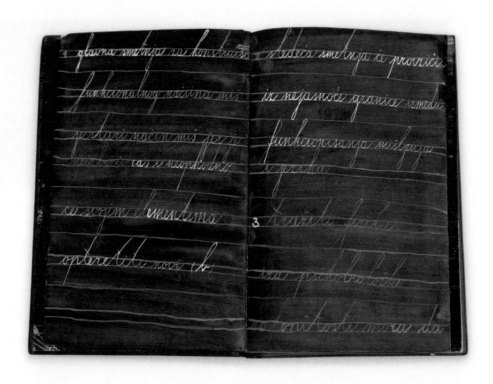

100   *enzyklopaediae* [encyclopedia]
        Painted notebook, 16.3 × 11,6 cm
        m.6 (1962)
"der geist [the spirit]
if one considers that the horse does not hold the spirit
and that man does,
then the difference is minor.
there is no doubt that it only concerns the size of their brains
and that the difference is of quantity.
both are matter which took shape
in a slightly different organization
there is no doubt that the horse's brain
in theory could evolve
into the same level as the human brain
ergo esprit niet."

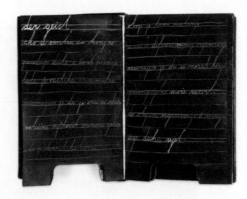

"small encyclopedia
of waste"

102   *antifreud*
Painted notebook, 16×12 cm
m.7 (1967)

"the mechanics of dreams"

104   *model fm*
Painted notebook, 32 sheets, 17 × 11.5 cm
m.7 (1970)

The abbreviation "fm" here stands for "funkcionalno mišljenje", the
functional thinking. Ilija and Mileva are the first names of Bašičević's
parents. Urashima Tarō is the name of the character in a japanese
legend (See p.15).

106   *hypotese f* [hypothesis f]
       Painted notebook, 19 × 11.3 cm
       m.9 (1978)

"the projects

1. hypothesis of two civilizations
2. hyp. hegel
3. hyp. of the ev(evolution) factor
4. hyp. chid
5. hyp.f (fumiš) [abbreviation for "functional thinking"]
6. hyp.e (energy)
7. hyp.r (revolution)"

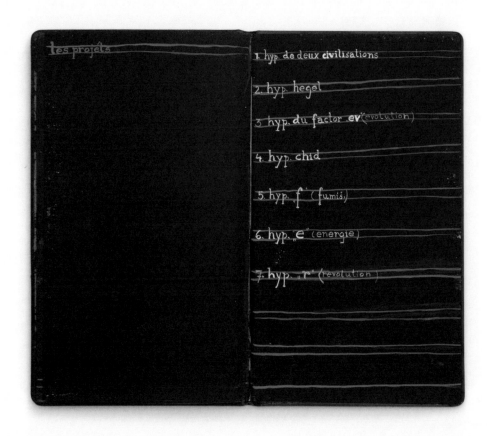

108 *theory of memory*
Painted notebook, 16 × 11 cm
m.7 (1976)

"dream
the progress of a dream is straight and continuous"

Editor: François Piron
Design: Laure Giletti
Authors: Ivana Bašičević Antić, Ješa Denegri, François Piron

This book is published in the aftermath of the exhibition *mangelos: miroirs noirs*, curated by François Piron at galerie frank elbaz, Paris, from November 9, 2013 to January 10, 2014. All exhibition views reproduced in the book are taken from this exhibition.

Unless otherwise mentioned, all works reproduced in the book belong to prof. Vojin Bašičević and are courtesy galerie frank elbaz, Paris.

The essay by Ješa Denegri was originally published in: *mangelos – Drugi o njemu*, Vojin Bašičević ed., Novi Sad, 1997, pp. 43–47

Translation from Serbian to English: Ivana Bašičević Antić, with the help of Courtney Donner (Gallery St. Etienne, NY)
From Croatian to French: Danka Sočić
From Croatian to English (mangelos' manifestos): Maja Šoljan
From French to English (text François Piron): Derek Byrne
Proofreading: Ivana Bašičević Antić, Thomas Boutoux
Photographs: Zarko Vijatović and Dusan Antić
Printing: Die Keure, Bruges

Thanks to Ivana Bašičević Antić, Frank Elbaz and Danka Sočić, and to Maria Ramos, head of the publication department, Fundação de Serralves, Porto.

Published by:
Paraguay Press
A division of castillo/corrales
80, rue Julien Lacroix
F-75020 Paris
www.paraguaypress.com

In association with:
galerie frank elbaz
66 Rue de Turenne
F-75003 Paris
www.galeriefrankelbaz.com

ISBN 978-2-918252-26-9
Dépôt légal: September 2014

112 *čovek to zvuči gordo ali ne funkcioniše*
[man, it sounds proud, but does not function]
Tempera on cardboard, 51 × 68 cm
m.7 (1963–70)

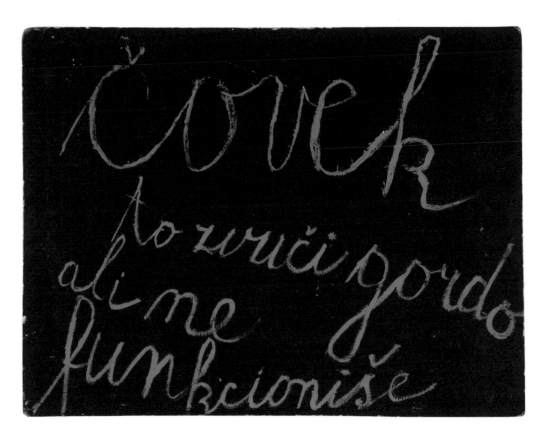